A PERFECT TIME

A
Perfect
Time

Richard Jones

COPPER CANYON PRESS

Publication of this book is supported by a grant from the National Endowment for the Arts and a grant from the Lannan Foundation. Additional support to Copper Canyon Press has been provided by the Andrew W. Mellon Foundation, the Lila Wallace–Reader's Digest Fund, and the Washington State Arts Commission. Copper Canyon Press is in residence with Centrum at Fort Worden State Park.

Library of Congress Cataloging-in-Publication Data
Jones, Richard, 1953–
A perfect time / Richard Jones
p.   cm.
ISBN 1-55659-068-7
1. Title.
PS3560.O52475P47 1994
811'.54 – DC20

COPPER CANYON PRESS
P.O. BOX 271, PORT TOWNSEND, WASHINGTON 98368

Acknowledgments:

Agni Review: The suit
Bluff City: Listening, The edge
Columbia Poetry Review: Cathedral, The temple
The Cream City Review: Pirandello's shirt
Green Mountains Review: The hermit
Great River Review: Ice
Onthebus: Leaving Los Angeles at last, The black snake,
    If I should die, The beginning
Osiris: Sacrifices
Pequod: My sister's garden
Poetry: Scars, Lanterns
The Seattle Review: The key
TriQuarterly: The black hat, The siesta, Dancing,
    The novel
Willow Review: The remedy

I would like to thank Copper Canyon Press for its faith
and dedication; DePaul University and the Illinois Arts
Council for grants which provided uninterrupted writing
time; the Calcagno family for their generosity; Mark
Arendt for his criticism and steadfast friendship; and my
family for their love.

for Antonella,
who turned out to be Laura

Contents

A PERFECT TIME

The key

This is my key to happiness,
the key to my room
in the *Hôtel du Paradis*.
The tireless Algerian
keeps the key behind the bar all day
to return to me at midnight
when I climb the narrow, winding stairs
with my pounding heart and loneliness.
The Algerian calls out *bonne nuit*;
I struggle with the broken lock.
A flimsy door, I could kick it down,
but when I am patient,
when, in my quietest voice,
I say *please*
it opens
and lets me in.
I turn on the light
and there is the cell of my dreary room –
the unmade bed, the open suitcase,
pitcher of stale water on the table.
I unlatch the window
and lean into the night
above torches of countless street lamps
and wild cars carving the boulevards
with blades of rushing lights.
I pray to the moon
rising above dark steeples,
ask the moon to translate for stars
listening unseen
beyond the city's dazzling lights.
Night after night,

sitting in my window, hungry and tired,
or pacing back and forth before my desk,
I have come to love
the one dim bulb
dangling from the ceiling on a thin black cord.
I have come to trust
the smallest illumination,
the tiniest omen,
wallpaper peeling away
to reveal origins and mysteries,
the hotel's ten thousand ghosts
and the sickly-sweet perfume of their bodies.
I've learned to write or read
to the music of motorcycles
roaring down tangled streets
or to fall asleep
long after midnight
to singing on sidewalks below.
Locking my door,
I turn out the light
to the distant wailing of sirens,
sit on my bed and consider my key,
a silver key with a worn yellow tag
the yellow of a dying daffodil,
room number 8 in red,
symbol of infinity
and my lucky number.
I've begun to believe
in the numerology of my birth –
August 8th, '53 –
three 8's in a row,

4

three affirmations
I will live forever.
I put the key under my pillow,
lie down,
cross my arms on my chest
and feel my beating heart
promising everything
if only I can wait until morning
when I wake
to the wild music
of all the city's church bells,
when I open my door
and lock it behind me,
when I bound down the winding stairs
that rush to the street,
to flower shops and cafés,
to the parks and river
and every stranger waiting
to ask my name
and greet me with a kiss –
all this,
my heart promises,
tomorrow,
after I've turned out the light
and slept on the narrow bed,
after I've awakened
and returned the key
to the smiling Algerian,
who waits behind the bar each morning
with my hunk of bread and my coffee,
my sugar and my cream.

5

Scars

This hollow of dead skin
the size of a coin
centered on my left shin
was a gift from the ocean –
the sharp blade of a shell
tore my leg open
to show the bone that carries me.
This ragged scar on my arm
I earned being introspective
walking in woods –
rusted barbed wire
ripped through my shirt to awaken me.
And the small white arc?
this tiny moon over my left eye?
– appeared from nowhere one day in the mirror.

My body reveals its history.
I would show you
invisible tokens
of sorrow and joy –
grief-scars and love-scars.
I remember crying all day
when my mother was
dying. I remember
Aunt Ruby, who took me in,
lifted me,
and covered my face with kisses.
I ran to the bathroom
and saw in the mirror
the bee-stings of her lipstick.

When I was a boy
I dreamed I could fly.
It was wonderful to soar
over my mother's house
with its locked doors
and shuttered windows!
Dreaming taught me
the body is nothing,
less than nothing,
less than a dream.

This morning I ate the fish
I caught last night.
I laid the fish on the kitchen counter –
an old, scarred, grandfather fish,
rainbow of flesh pale with age,
scales torn and dangling.
With a knife I cut off the head,
slit open the belly.
With my fingers I removed
brown and green entrails,
the tiny heart. From the sink,
the fish's ancient eye watched
as I ran the knife over the body,
the silver scales leaping in air.
I cooked the fish
in my grandfather's iron skillet,
battered and scratched from the years.
The hot oil smoked; the fish sizzled in the pan.
I love my body in the morning,

hunger raging inside me.
The body's hunger is beautiful.
I fill it with the wisdom of fish.
If I could fly, I'd visit my mother
in heaven. I'd hold her angel-hands
in my scarred mortal hands, and thank her
for giving me the world.

Lanterns

To believe in love,
I leave my house

before sunrise, my quest
sanctified by blue and gold

lights that burn
in tenement rooms

where a child wakes,
cries,

stirring a woman
who sleepily rises

to the child's hunger,
unbuttoning her nightshirt

and drifting down the hall
past the kitchen, where

beneath the halo
of the fluorescent light,

a man sits, drinking coffee,
waking to the particulars

of his existence –
woman, baby, radiator knocking

the chill from the room
as he bends like one in prayer

to lace his boots,
as he leaves to become

one of many men and women
in dungarees and hardhats

moving forward, inch by inch,
with tractors and earthmovers,

working for weeks, months
to make a new road,

concentrating,
this day,

on one broken-up square of highway
and the task of making it smooth,

working patiently as monks
in a monastery courtyard,

monks raking pebbles
in ripples and waves

to achieve the semblance
of ever-changing sea,

suggesting the beauty
of everything in nature

blessed,
as all things are,

by the sky,
by ten thousand stars

faintly visible
beyond the lanterns

hanging from branches of cherry trees,
red paper lanterns that burn each evening,

lit sometimes by a novitiate,
sometimes by the master.

The mystery

It's not easy
now that I live in the city
to find a quiet wooded place
to meditate on death,
to sit in shade
and consider the mystery
that worried me as a child:
where do animals go to die?
When I was a boy I would lie
beneath maples and elms for hours,
studying sky
vanishing
beyond lush branches
rocking back and forth in wind.
When I was a boy
I'd wander hushed woods all day
in search of the black snake
coiling into a question mark
one last time
to die...but it's not easy
here in the city's forest preserve
when cyclists race by on concrete paths
through woods into crowded parking lots
where picnickers feast on sandwiches
from trunks of cars in the blazing noon.
Here I'm tempted to forget death
and drink with these noisy families,
to ask for a deviled egg
or a piece of fried chicken
and, in return, quote a line of poetry
among the parked cars and folding tables –

but looking at their faces
I only think of lines that grieve.
If I'm in search of the mystery's answer,
why observe
the pair of kissing lovers
strolling hand-in-hand from the parking lot
into tall grass on the hill?
Look at them
taking off their clothes
on the bed
of their red-checked blanket,
oiling each other's body
tenderly in the sun.
Lovers know no grief.
Only children
search the woods
for the burial place of deer,
muddy graves of raccoons,
bones of herons hanging in branches,
tortoise shells lodged
in mossy hollows of rotten logs.
I consider these things
as I lie against a willow by the lake
and nap. When I wake, two men in a rowboat
are fishing just off shore, quiet and serious
in the last evening light.
They do not see me. I could be a deer
or fox come down to the water
for one last drink.
It is almost dark. Everyone
is gone. Now wild teenagers

arrive in vans, slamming doors,
parading toward the lake, carrying a box
of loud music that drowns their voices,
carrying their young bodies through darkness
to the lake's black water
where the moon, too,
will extinguish itself before dawn.
I look through the veil of willow branches
at evening's first star.
From this private, hidden place,
this shaded retreat,
the cries of teenagers
baptizing themselves in the forest's lake
grow distant and remote.
I remember when I was little,
afraid of wind in trees at night.
My Aunt Ruby would hold me
and rock me against her breast.
I knew then the simple answer:
animals know
when it is time to die.
They leave their own kind
and wander off
in search of a tranquil place to rest,
a serene wood pierced by a perfect ray of moonlight.

Ice

1. The Gift

The iceman –
taciturn, unshaven, his face
weathered and gray –
wore a gray felt hat
with the brim turned down,
a black band of sweat around the crown
dignified
by a small green feather.
I fed sugar cubes to the brown draft-horse
that pulled his heavy wagon up our hill
while my aunt fetched her beaded purse.
My aunt had no need of ice:
she owned a Frigidaire.
Ice was a strange and frivolous gift
she bought for me
those long, hot summer afternoons in the South.
The iceman dropped
her quarter in his apron,
pulled on thick, scarred leather gloves
and jerked down fiercely
on a rusted handle,
cold smoke rushing out the thick black door.
With heavy silver tongs
he dropped a block of burning ice in my hands;
I carried the ice up my aunt's flowered walk
and sat all day in the shade of a tree
just to watch it melt.
Leaning close to the clean-smelling chill,
I stared into the core of frozen water,

my hands cupping its sides,
consulting the crystal,
waiting for the mystery
of my life that summer
to reveal itself, my future
written by the iceman's tongs
in lacy veins that ran to the heart of the ice
and resembled, I realize, the filigrees of frost
on the window I'm looking through now.

2. *Climbing*

Outside – Chicago, January – a woman
hurries down the middle of the street,
head down against wind and snow.
Where is she going
so early on a Sunday morning?
What is she rushing toward?
I drop another ice cube into my glass
and drink to six A.M.
Up all night, I read a novel
about mountain climbing in Europe,
the skill it takes to survive
with pitons, hammers, and ropes.
The heroes are two men
who have grown to love each other,
as friends who risk their lives together
sometimes do. I confess
I have never climbed a mountain.
Friends out West tell me
the gentle rounded hills

of the ancient Blue Ridge
aren't really mountains at all:
no looming icy summits,
no dangerous impossible heights.
Once, after my divorce,
I hiked all day with my father
to the highest peak in Virginia.
He dressed that day
as if we were going to dinner –
blue coat, tie, oxfords.
I offered to trade shoes,
and halfway up, sitting on a log, we did.
The trail through the woods
opened onto jagged outcroppings of rock,
a clear autumn afternoon,
trees dying into brilliant colors
throughout the Shenandoah.
We sat on the cliff's edge.
His feet dangled in my tennis shoes;
my feet dangled in his oxfords.
The sky melted into the valley.
When I think of my father,
I think of the mountain
and wearing his slick-soled oxfords.
Walking the trail back down in the dark,
I slipped and he grabbed my hand.
The long hike up
he never complained,
though climbing in oxfords
must have been like climbing a mountain of ice,
like the mountain in the novel

I read all night, imagining
my father and me
on the icy face of a mountain in France,
our lives tied together by ropes.

3. *The Window*

This morning
in the first gray light
anyone who cared
could watch the dirty city slowly vanish
dreamlike into a snowstorm,
snow falling
on the tracks of the woman who passed.
Now snow falls
on the memory of her.
I was five the summer
I was sent to live with my aunt
where the draft-horse and ice wagon
climbed our gently sloping street,
leaving a trail of water
drying in the sun
 – just as my warm hand
leaves a trail of water
as it brushes the icy window clear.

The black hat

What should I do with the black hat
of the burglar who tried to break in
today? It was noon. I was in the basement
doing laundry
when he kicked in the back door.
I yelled, "Son of a bitch!"
He took off down the alley –
muscular, tall, younger than I.
For a block I chased him
but gladly lost him in the shadows,
then ran home, breathless,
and with shaking hands called the police.

When my house is burglarized,
they take my Walkman,
cameras, little things
they can carry and sell on the street.
I come home to my walls
ravaged with gang signs,
crowns and crosses
like the ones spray-painted in the alley.

"Gang signs
don't mean anything,"
the police said, looking around the house.
"Thieves throw blame on enemies."
What cops want
"is a detailed description –
age, height, race – "
of the man who disappeared down the alley.
To prove the thief's existence,

I introduced as evidence
the black hat
that flew off his head
when he ran.
"Keep it," they said,
"a souvenir,"
tearing their report from the pad.

I'm going to wash the hat,
wear it to work tomorrow.
I'll wear it to keep the sun out of my eyes
mornings when I weed the garden.
In the black hat
I'll look like a carpenter
as I repair the broken door.

Because I don't want to dream
about thieves at night,
I'll wear the black hat
in bed. I'll read Hikmet
and memorize the poem
in which he refuses to wear a hat
until everyone owns a hat.

I'll write a poem called "The Black Hat"
in the form of an epistle
or prayer,
pin my poem to the hat
along with the police report,
and hang the hat
where anyone can steal it –

in the tree branching out
over the alley's crosses and crowns.

"The Black Hat" –
inspired by the man who would rob me,
dedicated to the god
of thieves.

If I should die

If I should die this afternoon
who will take care of my dog?
Who will let her out this evening
and walk her twice around the block,
letting her stop now and then to sniff
an especially delicious turd
some other dog has left behind
just for her, a gift
hidden among leaves and tall grass
that she discovers
like a little girl at an Easter egg hunt?
Like a little girl, she needs someone to feed her.
Who will fill her red bowl with the bone-shaped feed
that smells of old socks, her favorite fragrance,
lovely aroma, gourmet that she is?
And who will howl with her at the moon at midnight
in the backyard as I do? Who will get down
on all fours, snarling by the back gate
at ghosts and thieves?
Who will bury his nose in snow or dirt or mud?
Who will walk in circles, curl on the old pillow,
dream the dream of the dog –
as I do, night after night,
lying on my back, my snout and whiskers twitching,
my eyes opening and closing,
my paws trembling, my legs shuttling back and forth?
Dreaming like a dog,
I chase whatever it is I want
but never catch in life,
though, in my dreams, like a dog, I do –
I catch it and bite down hard;

it can't get away;
I'm devouring it now, whatever it is,
whatever it was I wanted
all my life
and begged for
every day
like a dog.

The remedy

Tonight
I'm cooking tomato soup
in my yellow pot,
asking basil and a dozen cloves of garlic
to cure my pneumonia.

This morning,
appealing to the earth
to nurse me back to health,
appealing to the summer sun hot on my back
to burn away the cold gray clouds
gathered in my lungs,
I shambled to the garden,
filled my wicker basket
with vegetables and herbs,
and slowly, weakly,
pulled weeds
grown wild these long weeks of illness.
I despise weeds
as I despise pneumonia.
I stood among the chrysanthemums in my red robe
     and dared
weeds or death to mess with me.
I have two hands that aren't afraid to get dirty
and a knife that chops basil and celery.
I have a blender to puree tomatoes.
I know two Spanish onions who weep
over my feeble body,
who are willing to die
that I may live.

All day the soup simmered. All day
I opened cupboards and cabinets,
mixing elixirs, tonics,
relying on secret potions
and herbal concoctions
to cure me of all my diseases –
angelica for ills of my body,
valerian for ills of my mind,
the heart-shaped leaves of the pansy
to heal a broken heart.
To dispel dark thoughts
I rubbed my temples with lavender oil
and smeared crushed mint on my forehead.
I cast spells,
devising words of a vow
not to dwell on the past
or happiness I've known.
Sitting in my father's chair,
plucking honeysuckle flowers
made me remember
innocence
and drinking sweet nectar
drop by drop
made me forget
ruined cities
and my worn leather suitcase
filled with the willow branches
of my bitterness
and the chicory
of my anger.
Following doctor's orders –

while the yellow pot dozed and dreamt on the stove –
I slept in the sunroom all afternoon
like Rimbaud's dead soldier beside the brook,
the bullet hole in his heart like a blossom.
But unlike the soldier,
toward evening
I rose again.

The soup simmers on the stove,
aroma of garlic and basil
perfuming the house.
Like a French chef,
I lift the lid of my yellow pot with a flourish,
dip my spoon,
taste the tomatoes, smack my lips,
add spices –
dill, black pepper, sugar, cilantro –
working by intuition,
adding a little white wine
and a dash of tabasco
to cure the blues
that come with pneumonia.
Tonight there's almost nothing
left of my voice,
and yet it makes me happy,
here in my kitchen,
to sing a song
about the country
and gardens laid out
in tight little squares
like sonnets. It makes me happy

when I devote a verse
to lush gardens
that spring up like hope
on abandoned lots
in dying cities.
Tonight, delirious
with fever and exhaustion,
I stare into the black heart
of the kitchen window vivid with visions
of old men and old women in broad-brimmed hats
opening heaven's rickety garden gate
and walking through the country of air
to bring me gifts –
flowered aprons full of tomatoes.

Seven weeks
the Spanish moss
of pneumonia has hung
in the branches of my lungs;
seven weeks I've been
unable to get out of bed.
But tonight
in the kitchen in my smelly red robe,
stirring the yellow pot with a wooden spoon,
tonight
I curse infirmity
and celebrate the dignity
of slowly dying gardeners
who each day water onions
or plant flowers for sweethearts.
Like pulling weeds,

it makes me feel good to forgive the wasted
healthy days of youth,
to know that tomorrow
I'm going to wake and work again,
harvesting what the earth has promised,
daring the weeds, daring death.
I repeat: I've got two hands
unafraid of dirt.
I curse darkness.
I spit on the night that devours me.
I pour my bowl of soup
and recite this poem,
this magic,
this incantation cleaving sickness from
health. I open the door
and carry my bowl to my table in the garden,
blue-white moonlight
dusting my skin like pollen.
In the night-sweet air,
I fold my hands in prayer
and say grace, giving thanks
for tomatoes and herbs,
chrysanthemums and moonlight,
asking to live
a while longer in this body,
this body I bless at every meal,
crossing it with one hand,
feeding it with the other.

The suit

I am hungry
and have an hour,
so I stop at the corner diner
across from the railroad tracks
alongside Rosewood Cemetery.
I hesitate in the doorway
as a train rolls past
with its litany of empty windows,
wondering if the lunch waitress
is wearing her red hair pulled back
or letting it fall in her eyes.
Inside, I take off my suitcoat,
fold it, notice how the lining shines
like silk inside a coffin.
In the red vinyl booth
with the jukebox on the wall,
I flip through songs,
reading titles I'd forgotten,
remembering lyrics
as if they were poetry....
                           The waitress
never looks at me;
tapping her pen on her pad
she asks if I want more time
and waits to write whatever I say.
I order and eat
black bean soup
doused with hot sauce
before asking for the daily special –
turkey and mashed potatoes and carrots,
tossed green salad,

coffee and chocolate pie.
Halfway through dessert,
I retrieve a newspaper
drying on a steaming radiator.
As I sip my coffee,
my friend's obituary
smudges and dirties my hands.
I think of him yesterday –
his closed eyes,
his body dressed in suit and tie
lying among the flowers,
my friend who never wore a suit.
How strange to see
the mystery of his existence
reduced to nothing
but a few words
written by someone who never saw him,
the song of his long life
brief as a poem.
I ask the waitress
                    what time is it?
as I pay the bill.
Writing the total on her little pad,
she says *quarter to two.*
I want her eyes to look into mine
but it's terrifying
to really look at someone
and risk small stars of pain
igniting in their eyes,
though sometimes
looking into eyes can be

just like making love.
I look down.
I look at my suitcoat,
shining,
and put it on.
My suit makes me feel
italicized.
March seventeenth. Two o'clock.
I leave the diner
and walk through the tunnel
under the railroad embankment,
wishing a train would fly overhead
like thunder, like wild clouds of glory.
But there is only the long silence of empty tracks.
And on the other side,
a few cars driving slowly through the rainbow archway,
the entrance to Rosewood Cemetery.

The black snake

If only I could make amends
for the black snake I killed.

My wife was afraid
of snakes getting into our house
through the pipes.
I was teetering on a ladder,
painting the tallest part of the house,
the gable where a lightning rod stabs the sky,
when I saw the black snake flowing
toward the open cellar door.
I climbed down,
ran to the shed for the shovel.
When I returned,
the snake was half-hidden beneath dead leaves
between the house and the flowering forsythia.
Imagine the black snake recoiling
before the raised blade –

I buried the snake in the orchard.
That was the last summer
my wife and I lived
in harmony.
The ensuing years brought
poverty,
the death of my nephew,
our divorce. If anyone asked
I'd tell them I still love
the house we lived in,
the way she laughed,
the animals that came down

from the mountains at night.
But it's no good
to talk about the black snake.
Nothing I say can change what happened.
I killed it because I loved her.

The beginning

I'll never forget the night
the phone rang
and my father told me,
"Andrew is dead."
A summer evening in Earlysville....
Sky beginning to purple
over the Blue Ridge....
I was in the living room
dancing
to some music I can never listen to
again.
I was doing the watusi, the skate,
even stranger dances I invented
those long evenings
of separation
from my wife, the woman
I was beginning to love at last.
Six clowns hung on the wall –
faces my nephew had painted
and given as a gift,
some smiling, some crying,
one with closed eyes
opening his green lips
to scream.
I had to stop dancing,
lift the needle from the black grooves
circling endlessly,
turn away from the clowns
and walk through the house
past things my wife had left behind.
I walked through the kitchen

and looked out at the mountains,
the beautiful evening,
the world I loved
dying into the dark.
I picked up the phone.
Heard my father's voice.
And closed my eyes,
closed them forever,
though the stars were just beginning
to come toward me –
small bright needles.

Sacrifices

All winter the fire devoured everything –
tear-stained elegies, old letters, diaries, dead flowers.
When April finally arrived,
I opened the woodstove one last time
and shoveled the remains of those long cold nights
into a bucket, ash rising
through shafts of sunlight,
ash swirling in bright, angelic eddies.
I shoveled out the charred end of an oak log,
black and pointed like a pencil;
half-burnt pages
sacrificed
in the making of poems;
old, square handmade nails
liberated from weathered planks
split for kindling.
I buried my hands in the bucket,
found the nails, lifted them,
the phoenix of my right hand
shielded with soot and tar,
my left hand shrouded in soft white ash –
nails in both fists like forged lightning.
I smeared black lines on my face,
drew crosses on my chest with the nails,
raised my arms and stomped my feet,
dancing in honor of spring
and rebirth, dancing
in honor of winter and death.
I hauled the heavy bucket to the garden,
spread ashes over the ground,
asked the earth to be good.

I gave the earth everything
that pulled me through the lonely winter –
oak trees, barns, poems.
I picked up my shovel
and turned hard, gray dirt,
the blade splitting winter
from spring. With hoe and rake,
I cultivated soil,
tilling row after row,
the earth now loose and black.
Tearing seed packets with my teeth,
I sowed spinach with my right hand,
planted petunias with my left.
Lifting clumps of dirt,
I crumbled them in my fists,
loving each dark letter that fell from my fingers.
And when I carried my empty bucket to the lake
    for water,
a few last ashes rose into spring-morning air,
ash drifting over fields
dew-covered
and lightly dusted green.

My sister's garden

She hated going into the garden alone.
The garden, with high grass choking the baby's breath
and weeds crowding the daisies,
had become a recrimination.
She would walk out each morning with her mug of
    hot coffee,
her heart full of hope,
and the garden – wild, untended, its red and yellow
    blossoms
lost in tall green shoots of burst seed tendrils –
would be a reminder that yesterday,
and the day before,
and for all the days of spring,
she had done nothing, had forsaken the work
of weeding and watering,
splitting of roots and bulbs,
mulching, the matching of colors –
purple of iris against pink of azalea.
What *had* she done
those long, cool spring afternoons?
What had she done yesterday
when the sun rose and the heat came?
She had lounged in her chair in the garden and waited
for the sun to come around the tree
and bathe her face with light.
She had dreamed of the time
when she first entered the yard,
when the garden was only an idea,
something growing in her imagination.
Taking paper, she had drawn plans,
herbaceous borders, banks of flowers,

small hills of camellias,
the far wall covered with honeysuckle and clematis.
She had taken a spade and turned soil,
making an outline, lifting dirt, a curving line
rolling away in a black wave,
the blade of the shovel whispering
each time she leaned the weight of her life
on her boot and pushed down.
And how many days passed
kneeling in dirt with marigold seeds, daffodil bulbs,
small pots of perennials she'd bought at the garden store?
...Now, flowers come up year after year,
bloom in spite of her.
Bulbs open
and the green tongues of their longing kiss the air,
buds opening
in the sun like memory,
a memory of pain
she bows to and smells like a flower
whose fragrance stays for days,
memory
the garden she may enter at any moment
simply by opening her door and stepping outside
to lose herself
in the world growing wild around her,
the world with all its blossoming and perfumes,
its dazzling light and dew, the world
that is ten thousand worlds –
small plateaus of leaves,
the rope of each stem,
the dusty cloud of every petal –

a beautiful web in which she, now,
has become only the smallest part
and the only part
that knows and feels and believes
in pain, but also knows
she, too, must
blossom.

Listening

It was all I could give –
my eyes two drops of rain,
my hands on the table two sleeping birds,
my chest turned toward you with no shield,
the two wounds of my ears,
my slow-breathing silence,
my head slowly nodding
a flower heavy with dew,
the sun coming from behind a cloud,
a piece of light
falling on the table between us like bread,
falling on hands, our hands touching,
this moment of my listening,
this dark time of your voice, saying,
"this flower, this light, this bread,"
your words a piece of bread
you break in two
and share.

Leaving Los Angeles at last

I'm stealing my friend's Volkswagen,
pushing it out of his driveway while he's sleeping,
rolling it down the hill toward Silver Lake
to get the beat-up old beauty started.
Mine is a long, dangerous journey
requiring a stolen car, an assumed name,
the mind of a thief, and the heart of a sinner.
I'm saying good-bye to Los Angeles at last,
to movie stars and *La Casa Bonita*,
to the *Times* and Hare Krishnas.
I'm ripping the suit off my back
as if it were in flames
and throwing my shoes out the window –
two dead birds on the side of the road.
I'm flying down the Hollywood to the Santa Monica,
the 405 to San Diego,
smuggling what I need to survive
in Bibles hollowed out with a razor –
tapes of Bach and Miles Davis,
photographs of my beautiful childhood
and photographs of the agony
of my youth and first loves.
I'm hanging a ribbon of thorns
from the rear-view mirror,
turning up the radio
and singing "Unchain My Heart" with Ray Charles,
improvising, changing the words, making the song
an anthem for martyrs and saints.
After crossing the border
I'll travel by night,
sleeping by day on the empty beach

or in caves in the mountains above the desert.
So no one will suspect me,
I'll wear a serape like the old Robert Bly,
a white linen suit like Faulkner.
I'll master the art of disguise,
walk with a limp,
speak with an odd, hard-to-place accent –
could be French, could be Romanian.
In the small villages,
with my sunglasses and zinc oxide,
my bermudas, straw hat, and camera,
I'll look like a Swedish tourist.
I'll abandon the Volkswagen
and slip through Mexico and Honduras,
be tempted by Belize,
but will lose myself for good
in Ecuador or Uruguay.
I'll take a room above a quiet taverna
and lie in bed all day, remembering.
The doors of my balcony will be open
to let in dreams or memories,
the curtains – if there are curtains – blowing
in the breeze from the ceiling fan.
And perhaps, in Paraguay or Peru,
I'll be forgiven. I'll enter
the little white adobe church,
the one with the painted wooden Madonna
grieving in her green and yellow gown,
silverblue drops of paint on her cheeks.
Kneeling at the altar,
light pouring through open windows like grace,

I'll bow before the priest,
kiss the hem of his robe,
kiss his bare ankles and feet.
Finally I'll begin to weep,
knowing at last the hungry flames
of the candles have devoured
whatever dream was meant for me.
Beyond prayer, beyond blessing,
there will be nothing
for the priest to do
but bow his head and watch me cry,
laying his hand on my shoulder
as if I were his long-lost son
and he my father.

The novel

For two days I've been crying,
from Paris to Rome, from Rome to Palermo,
weeping and sobbing here on the train
over a nineteenth-century novel.
Some paragraphs are so beautiful
I lean my head against the window
while villages fly past
like books I'll never open.
When I come to the last few sentences
of an exquisitely painful chapter,
I drop the novel in my lap
or crush it to my chest
and cover my face with my hands,
trembling and shaking.

People on the train
don't know what to do with me
or why I rock back and forth
clutching my book and sniffling.
From Paris to Rome,
the French hated me for crying.
They blew smoke in my face
and cursed me in their beautiful language.
But now, along the Amalfi Coast,
beside blue waters and grottos,
the great hearts of the Italians
take pity –
they offer me water,
offer me wine.

We open the window and smoke together
until I compose myself.
These are my five angels –
a baker from Napoli,
a nun,
young Rafael the fisherman,
and an old married couple,
young lovers once,
now shrunk to the size of children.
The baker from Napoli speaks for them all,
asking what troubles me.
The five Italians lean forward.
For a long moment I'm silent,
looking down at the novel
that is the story of my life,
a secret between the author and me.
I am the hero,
and though I am brave,
indefatigable, loyal, intrepid,
I cannot bear to hear it all again.
My story is blessed with moments of joy,
but they are brief
and flicker like distant stars.
The author knows
truth is tragic.
Relentless, tireless, devoid of sympathy,
he talks and talks
like the heartbeat of time
while I grow weaker and weaker,
no longer a hero,
but a boy again,

weeping when my mother falls ill in the castle,
weeping when Fabiana, my little sister,
is abducted by thieves and gypsies
and forced to dance naked
before a fire in the camp of the Hussars.

The Italians are waiting.
I look up at the luggage rack,
suitcases and plastic bags
piled precariously over their heads.
I look out the window at blue doors and green doors
of whitewashed houses built on the edges of cliffs
here at the foot of the famous volcano.
When I finally lean forward, I whisper,
slowly, so they will understand,
"My wife died,
and my child,
horribly,
in an accident,
in America, America,
an accident in America,
my wife and child,
morto, morto."
The Italians lean back,
overcome, delighted,
crossing themselves,
everyone talking at once.
My confession makes them happy,
makes them hungry.
They bring out sandwiches,
pears, olives, and cheese.

We feast all afternoon
until sated and sleepy,
until they all lean back in their worn red seats
and the baker, with his hands, asks,
"And now?"
I tell them I'll retreat
to an island to rest,
recover, renew my life
again. I tell this
in broken Italian
and simple French,
using only the present tense and infinitives.
I employ words I remember
from German and Spanish,
I speak English when the story
becomes complex and difficult
though the words themselves
are plain and simple.
My five angels understand best
when I make wild and mysterious gestures
with my hands, when I beat my fist
against the coffin of my heart
or fall silent,
and they have only to look in my face
to see how far I've come,
to see my heart is broken.

II.

As the sun goes down,
I tell them a story,

make them swear never to repeat it,
telling the story only in English
to emphasize feeling over fact.
"I saw something very strange
today in Rome," I tell them.
"I was passing the time between trains
in the gardens of the Villa Borghese,
sitting on a bench, eating ice cream.
A man walked toward me down the gravel path
near the stalls of the *carabinieri*.
Smartly dressed, handsome, he seemed
carefree, tossing keys in his left hand
and humming under the linden trees.
A moment later a woman rushed through the gate,
running toward him,
awkwardly carrying her coat
as her shoulder bag bounced and knocked against her.
She was screaming; he ignored her
and kept walking.
I thought perhaps that he had said something to her
on the street before entering the garden
or had been forward on a crowded bus,
that she came now for revenge,
to defend her honor,
that he would feign innocence,
swear he'd never touched her.
When the woman caught the man,
she dropped her coat and bag,
spun him around
and beat him with her fists,
scratching his face,

49

clawing his eyes.
And the man did nothing
except close his eyes
and hold on to his broken glasses,
absorbing the blows like a saint,
like a martyr.
It was then I realized
he loved her,
she was his wife,
that she too must have loved him very much
to attack him this way in a public park.
She beat him until there was no good in it,
until he turned away
and, his back to her, began to weep.
She stepped back, yelling,
hurling questions at the wall of his back.
He turned. Unable to meet her eyes,
he said something so softly
only she could hear.
Then she took a step forward,
wanting to hit him again,
raised her fists,
but fury had left her
and the man walked away
down the path in sorrow.
She followed,
but not before she bent to pick up
the keys he had dropped in the dirt,
the keys he would have forgotten
and lost
had she not been there."

I ask the Italians if they understand.
No one says a word. Now,
I tell them, I will finish the story,
this parable, this little novel,
reminding them of their vow
never to repeat it.

"The man and woman walked to the stables
where they studied the horses of the *carabinieri*.
The proud horses – usually aloof and haughty –
returned the lovers' gaze with patient brown eyes,
tossing their heads sympathetically
like priests.
                          And though I had no right
to follow the lovers with my ice cream and notebook,
though the lovers' novel was written in Italian,
I eavesdropped as the horses spoke,
as horses in Italian novels sometimes do,
forgiving the man his infidelity,
the woman her inability to forgive.
The horse-priests said,
La passione è difficile,
and offered themselves
as models of discipline.
The horses said their lives were a novel
full of grain and wind and sweat.
They told of men in blue uniforms
who arrive with the light each dawn
to wash and brush them,
bringing fresh straw.
The horses said they love each day,

galloping through the woods
or walking slowly by the villa's open windows
so their riders can admire the lovely sculptures,
the horrible *Rape of Persephone*,
the terrible *Apollo and Daphne*.
The horses said they don't understand
the human love
of stories in marble and bronze.
They understand only
that each day as they enter the woods
with light falling through trees,
with leaves under their hooves,
their hearts become so full they think
if they don't die right then
they will surely live forever.
And when the horses fell silent
and bent their heads to the sweet water
flowing fresh down the long wooden trough,
the lovers turned away,
perhaps toward home,
where they would make love,
touching each other gently and with respect,
then with increasing passion and need,
healing one another simply
with their love."

In the compartment,
the baker, nun, fisherman,
and tiny old couple
listen to each word,
leaning forward when I whisper,

nodding at a word they understand –
carabinieri, Bernini.
But I am finished talking;
I will say nothing more in English.
But they don't know that yet,
and watch me and wait to see if the story continues.
When I finally lower my head,
open my book
and continue reading,
they don't wait for my tears;
they argue over the meaning of my story,
yelling at one another,
waving hands, interpreting,
translating, revising, editing, embellishing,
digressing
into the mystery
of lives they have observed,
adding their own emotions
and personal histories
as if they've comprehended everything I've said
and no longer need to consult me,
talking among themselves now
as if I had disappeared.

III.

Just before midnight,
we take turns in the w.c.
with our toothbrushes and our washcloths.
When the coach lights go out,
the nun vows to watch over me

as I finish my book by flashlight,
but she's a tired angel
and falls asleep in a minute.
The old couple curl
on their seats like two cats –
they're that small.
The baker snorts and snores,
hands on his belly,
face white as flour in the moonlight.
But Rafael, the fisherman,
is too young to sleep.
He stands outside in the corridor,
admiring the moon and moonlit water,
thinking,

I will tell my friends
what I heard and saw on my journey.
I will sit in my uncle's café
and my cousin will bring wine and glasses.
We'll drink to the moon
bathing the rocky coast of our village
and to spells the moon casts on fish
we catch in our nets at dawn.
I will tell my friends about the strange American
and how fine it is to stay up all night
admiring the moon,
admiring the moonlit water.
And I will tell them how,
when the entire train was dreaming
except for the American
hidden behind his book and flashlight,

I saw an old man in the next compartment
sitting across from his daughter,
admiring her as she slept,
tenderly, secretly watching her,
biting his knuckle now and then,
so astonished was he by her beauty.

Cathedral

Songbirds live
in the old cathedral,
caged birds bought at the street market
and freed as a kind of offering.
Now doves and finches and parakeets
nest in the crooks of the nave's highest arches,
roosting on the impossibly high
sills of stained glass windows,
looking down into the valley of the altar
as if from cliffs.

Twice a day, you'll hear them singing:
at dawn
when the blue light
of angels' wings
and the yellow light of halos
flood into their nests to wake them;
and during mass
when the organ fills
the valley below with thunder.
These birds love thunder,
never having seen a drop of rain.
They love it when the people below stand up
and sing. They fly
in mad little loops
from window to window,
from the tops of arches
down toward the candles and tombs,
making the sign of the cross.

If you look up during mass
to the world's light falling
through the arms of saints,
you can see birds flying
through blue columns of incense
as if it were simple wood smoke
rising from a cabin's chimney
in a remote and hushed forest.

The white star of hope

At the height of the storm's fury,
I lay in bed,
feverish, delirious,
willing at last to surrender
all my illusions
of happiness
and pass from the world unnoticed....

Outside the window –
towering thunderheads,
anvil clouds,
and a white flower with five pointed petals
blooming on the hill beyond my window,
silhouetted –
when the lightning flashed –
between sea and sky.
Delicate as a lily,
it was the only flower
left alive on the barren island,
the only flower to survive
African storms
and winds sweeping down from the Alps.

If I was going to die,
this flower –
this little White Star of Hope –
would be my last religion,
more beautiful than the earthly rose,
more graceful than the spiritual poppy.
I put all my faith

in five white petals tossing in the wind,
closed my eyes
and slept.

On the third day, my fever broke.
I drank some onion soup,
felt my strength returning.
According to the laws of my new religion,
I opened my door and weakly climbed the hill
to offer a stone of thanks
but the White Star of Hope was gone.

Had my flower walked
across the water, across the mountains
to the door of another deathbed?
Had I truly seen the flower?
Or was it only a dying man's dream,
a simple vision that visits souls
after terror passes
in the final hours of peace?

Then I saw the clouds, too,
had vanished.
The storms had passed;
the sea was calm.
The sea and sky will change
and remain the same
forever,
as I shall,

wandering in the mountains,
steadfast in my faith.
Along roads scarring the valley
or shepherd paths climbing the hills,
I kneel by the wayside
and construct an altar
for other weary travelers
in need of a place to worship,
as I was in need, sick and dying,
propped up on my pillow, studying
the White Star of Hope through the window.

Saved by a flower,
I now build altars of stone,
small mounds of rock
bearing a twig
or a bramble
studded with five torn pieces of paper
on which holy words are written –
hope, faith, love, everlasting
glory –
torn pages
tossing in the wind,
a white star of hope
covered with salt and dust.

Mortification of the flesh

The words come from nowhere
like stars so bright, so perfectly constellated
they seem an unmistakable command
clearly translated from the unknowable
language of God:
dive off the cliff in the dark.
After a month at my desk,
lost in the world of the spirit,
lost in the world of the mind,
I unbutton my shirt, feel
a shiver of cold air on my chest.
For the first time in days I listen
to the storm raging outside.
I open my door and rain rushes in,
scattering across the floor like blowing sand.
I leave my desk with its bright light and books
and start out blindly down the hill across the meadow,
abandoning my shoes,
stumbling as I take off my pants,
rain lashing my body, wind punishing me,
brambles and briars tearing my skin.
I climb rocks like a goat
to a ledge at the end of the world,
the face of the cliff
ravished white by lightning –
the voice says *dive!*
Below me, the sea
throws itself on the rocks,
unable to bear living forever.
Dive off the cliff!
Mortified, my terror trapped

between rocks and waves and rain,
I take off my glasses,
ultimate gesture of the lonely intellectual,
and scream like a madman, a lunatic angel,
"I am the King of Sicily!
I am the Eight of Wands!
I summon the devil! I summon death!
I command the night to behold my body,
this glowing angel, this luminous chariot!"
My name married to thunder and wave,
I open my arms to the storm,
and leap,
my glasses in my hand.
I dive from the cliff like a hawk,
fly through the air like a falcon,
drop in the sea like a gull.
Salt of darkness, blanket of thunder,
distant explosions of waves.
Fierce currents rock me like a mother
but it's too late:
I'm dead.
I'm seaweed, salt,
an empty shell rolling over the desert of the ocean floor.
Like any drowned thing, my body
washes onto the shore of the world.
My hands bleeding,
my feet bleeding,
I crawl over knives of coral,
I lie on blades of rocks,
half human, half fish,
singing softly,

praising the mortal body,
honoring astonished flesh,
blessing rocks,
blessing furious waves,
giving thanks for wind and rain,
leaving them to struggle without me.
In the meadow, over the graves of my shoes,
I stand and bless the storm, bless bloodied hands,
cliff and lightning
and the sea from which my life is resurrected,
my spirit redeemed.
Climbing the hill,
my face in the rain, my feet in the thorns,
I put on my glasses and see
the stutter of a yellow light –
my door
banging open and shut in the wind,
the light from my desk
a beacon guiding me
back up the hill,
back to my house,
back to my pens and books.

The cave

After climbing the hill,
after leaving a trail
ragged as a scar
through thick yellow grass
and wild flowers wet with dew,
after basking all morning
like a lizard on a hot stone
high above the dazzling sea,
after squinting for hours
into bright, flawless, empty sky
until the sun had burned
every dream
from my sleepy eyes,
I foolishly thought
it would be easy
to turn from light
and enter the cave.
I thought
it would be nothing
to abandon my shadow
and marry darkness,
to descend into gloom
and suffer
the underworld's cold
murky tunnels
and narrow passageways.

The mouth of the cave
– sunstruck –
seemed the portal
to a secret temple

carved into the mountain
centuries ago, a temple
flooded with eternal light;
but the twisting tunnels I wandered
soon became a labyrinth,
the way uncertain,
as darkness
swept over my body
like black water,
like night sweeping through the cavernous
space between stars.
Lost,
my sightless hand
held out to whatever was there,
my foot inched forward in dust....

Finally,
I stopped,
placed my hand
on my pounding heart,
and listened
to the rush of each breath –
its echo
a quiet litany
whispered back by the void.
Then I understood
why I left
the green and yellow world,
why I abandoned
the day to live
in a temple

of darkness:
perfectly still,
quietly breathing,
hand on my chest,
I closed my eyes
and inhabited
the lightness of each moment,
the perfect union
of heartbeat and breath,
the miracle of the body
which is
and forever shall be
the poem
against loneliness and death,
world without end....

Eyes quieted
by darkness,
I turned
and began the slow
ascent,
trusting the path
of dust, trusting
the trembling world
to be there
– shimmering –
noon's bright promise
fulfilled
as the tunnel opened
into wide chambers
and dusky light,

walls adorned
with hieroglyphics
of carved hearts
and chiseled names,
hard floor littered
with broken bottles,
bits of clothing,
charred circles,
flashes of sunlight
and my shadow,
the black cross of my body,
breathing in, breathing out –
heart radiant at the mouth of the cave.

Pirandello's shirt

In spite of the black mask
and thin black mustache
painted on with magic marker,
I recognized Pirandello
when he climbed through my window,
meowing and curling up at my feet to nap.
Just one or two hunks of cheese,
a slice or two of prosciutto,
and he follows me everywhere
like a starving dog, racing past me
every night on the stairs
like an alley cat
anxious to watch the moon rise.
On the roof I dip some bread in wine –
I'm willing to share –
but his hunger is terrifying,
especially considering the fact
he's been dead fifty years.
We strike a bargain,
nothing to do with charity,
nothing to do with gifts:
I keep my bed,
he sleeps perched like an owl on the garden wall.
On Sunday mornings, he leads me
to the edge of the cliff.
We wait for the lone truck to roar
from the village down to the sea,
where the fishmonger opens his door
and throws dozens of fish back into the water.
Some are frozen in solid blocks
and sink to the bottom

like stones from a temple,
a carved frieze of fish.
Others break free and float on the surface,
glinting like knives.
I tell Pirandello I've never read his plays,
I want to know what he wants,
why he's come back.
If he has some message,
I demand to hear.
I threaten him, make a fist,
grab his shabby suit and shake him
until there's only a black shirt in my hand,
which I put on to fight the chill,
a shirt the color of night,
the shirt that will make me invisible
as I sit here for a thousand years
watching the rituals of hunger,
rituals of life and death,
birds flying, their savage symphony,
the dead caught in their beaks,
the dead hanging from their talons.

The hermit

I'm sleeping on my red-tiled roof,
a roof garden rich with bougainvillea
cascading like a waterfall over the ledge.
I'm sleeping between pots of pink geraniums
and boxes of blue forget-me-nots,
one ear to the silent world of my house,
one ear to heaven's white rush of stars.
Curled on my side like a dog,
I'm finally content –
my closed eyes two smiles,
fists under my chin two wild flowers
ready to blossom. Here beneath the stars,
I'm dreaming of the past, remembering
the house I slept in when I was young
and saying my first good-byes.
I see my mother in bed dying,
my father the pilot leaving again
to fly through the country of air.
I see myself washing happiness from my hands
in the cold stream that swept down our hill.
I'm drinking the clear water;
I'm slipping and getting my shoes wet.
I'm wading upstream into the forest,
seeking the place where a recluse dwells
by the din of a hidden waterfall.
From the doorway of his shack,
the old man watches me climb the rocky path.
Bearded, gaunt, wild from long years of solitude,
his fierce eyes fix on me
as I approach
and ask his name...

ask again....
But the hermit can't hear,
having lived long
by the deafening water.
All he hears
is an endless rush,
a sound like wind
or God.
He puts his finger to his lips
and says,

Shhh...
        listen –

Dancing

I'm dancing to drums of distant thunder,
my bare feet raising clouds of dust
on the dirt street in front of my house.
I'm dancing with the island's two bony dogs
and the harbor's thirteen starving cats.
I'm singing a song of thanks to the bat
eating the singing mosquitoes,
watching them all blindly diving
through the street lamp's yellow sea of light.
I'm crooning to the clouds
rushing in from the East,
asking if they speak English,
asking will they marry me.
Above the mountain, lightning flashes;
the sea turns itself to stone.
The sea thinks rain is an insult.
But I love the rain.
I love the rain on my face like a thousand kisses
when I'm dancing and the sky is black.
I love it even after I've been abandoned,
after the dogs are gone, the cats,
after the bat has flown back to its cave,
back to the heart of the mountain.
The door to my house is open,
my books spread out on the table.
The wind blows –
pages flutter, crazy with knowledge.
My notebook shuffles its pages,
looking for a poem about winter,
looking for a poem about death.
The house says, "Come in, it's cold,"

but I don't know if the house means
the storm
or its own yellow light.
So tonight, as the rain dies,
I keep dancing,
touching the world with my feet
here in the road
between my house and the raging sea.
My feet love stomping in the dust.
They love splashing in water.
Surely somewhere on earth
there must be a fire
where people are dancing,
dancing on coals,
preparing for the fire beyond.
Dirt road, muddy stream, circles danced around a fire –
all the same.
There's only one path to paradise:
my left foot – a cloud of dust,
my right foot – a mud puddle splashing!

The siesta

Everyone knows it's no use to wonder,
but after three cappuccinos
I can't help asking
as I lie down
beneath my arbor of fig trees and grape vines,
what would have happened
if I hadn't slept all summer?
And how will things change
if Antonella says yes?
Blue washes over the courtyard,
saying it doesn't matter.
Now and then, according to the whim
of the breeze, sunlight through
holes in my green heaven dazzles me.
I don't know which I love more,
the grape leaves like giant clover
or the two suits of the schizophrenic fig,
half its leaves shaped like clubs,
half like hearts or spades.
The doctor says rest.
Antonella says love.
But who can sleep
or pucker up for a kiss
when it's impossible to tell
if the vines' dark twisting alleys
and the branches' broad highways
are paths that lead to the empire's decline
or roads that lead to glory!

The temple

I'm building the temple
stone by stone,
raising statues of women,
raising statues of men.
I've constructed an altar
of oyster shells and olive branches.
Any peasant can make an offering –
rusty nails, bent and broken,
old keys that open nothing and go nowhere,
dead flowers, spent candles, poems.
My temple has no walls, no doors.
Sunlight flows between the columns.
All are welcome
to slip in and admire the moon,
or leave, if it's late and they must,
stealing across the meadow,
the hillside white with dew,
the city burning below,
knowing there is a god,
never looking back.

The edge

It doesn't have to be terrifying.
Sometimes it's simply curling your toes
over the end of the high dive,
bending your knees and lightly bouncing
up and down, as if your wings were fluttering.

Or it might be the moment when you're waiting –
dawn – at the border –
for the man in the blue uniform
to hand back your passport,
to say it's all right to leap
from the train to the platform.

And after the flying and the splash,
after you haul your bag up on your shoulder,
it's safe to say that before long
you'll come to the edge of *something*
and have to leap again.

Maybe it's someone you didn't see
by the pool, wearing a flowered bathing suit –
maybe the love of your life.
Or maybe it's a museum with one painting
that finally explains everything.

And even if death *is* waiting,
you can still love
the perfect fit of the doorknob
in your hand as you open the door.
You can still search for the immortal
painting and buy postcards of it

to send all over the world.
You can leap
and let the water hold you,
throwing one hand over the other,
hoisting yourself up
to dry your body in the sun.
You can lift your rucksack –
the road rolling away before you –
and walk on joyfully,
going forward, forever leaping,
loving the high dive as well as the bottom stair,
loving the held breath, loving the tired feet.

On suffering

Four in the morning in a quiet house
is like a clearing in a forest,
tranquil, serene, a perfect time
to ask forgiveness
or consider the future's empty face
rising like a new moon,
a good time
to rise from bed,
descend the stairs,
turn on the kitchen light
and warm some milk.
It's relaxing
to watch a pot of milk
slowly come to a boil.

At this hour,
it's easy to mourn
the infinitesimal world
of one's life,
the sad history of the heart.
Sitting on the side of my bed
sipping milk,
slipping out of my slippers,
I turn out the light,
lie down,
and consider the simplicity
of the beginning,
the first word,
light.

I once read
that milk,
warmed,
is a sedative.
Do you believe that?
Do you believe falling asleep
is a form of death?
Waking,
a resurrection?
Do you know what I think,
drifting off toward dawn?
If, in the garden of the world,
there's such a thing as suffering,
I have never suffered.

Book design and composition by John D. Berry, using Aldus PageMaker
5.0 and an Apple Macintosh IIvx. The type is Sabon, designed in 1966
by Jan Tschichold. Sabon is based on the types of Claude Garamond,
and was designed as a functional and elegant text type that could be
used simultaneously in hot metal on Monotype and Linotype typesetting
machines and for hand-setting in metal foundry type. This is Linotype's
digitized version of the typeface. Printed by Thomson-Shore, Inc.